Football Legend

Phil Kettle
illustrated by Craig Smith

Black Hills

Distributed in
the United States of America
by Pacific Learning
P.O. Box 2723
Huntington Beach, CA
92647-0723

Website:
www.pacificlearning.com

Published by Black Hill
(an imprint of Toocool Rules
Pty Ltd)
PO Box 2073
Fitzroy MDC VIC 3065
Australia
61+3+9419-9406

First published in the United States by Black Hills in 2004.
American editorial by Pacific Learning in 2004.
Text copyright © Phillip Kettle, 2001.
Illustration copyright © Toocool Rules Pty Limited, 2004.

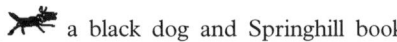 a black dog and Springhill book

Printed in China through Colorcraft Ltd, Hong Kong

ISBN 1 920924 07 8
PL-6209

10 9 8 7 6 5 4 3 2 1   08 07 06 05 04

Contents

Scott

Dog

Toocool

Chapter 1

The Super Bowl

It was the big day. The grand championship football game—the Super Bowl. My team, the Toocool Topdogs, was playing the Underdogs. I was the quarterback of the Topdogs. My friend, Scott, plays all the other positions.

We weren't sure who would play for the Underdogs. It could be Dog, or maybe Bert the Rooster.

I fixed my hair. I looked good. I always looked good.

I could see the stadium from the bathroom window. Rain was already falling. I could tell that the field would be wet and muddy. This would be a tough game. The Topdogs would need me more than ever.

I had taped a sign to my
bedroom door. It was written
in the team colors. It said
LOCKER ROOM, in big
bold letters.

My uniform was laid out.
I pulled on my pads, jersey,
pants, and socks. Then I tied on
my cleats as tight as I could.

I looked like a football star.
I imagined my picture on the
cover of sports magazines.
Toocool: Football Legend.

I headed for the back door.
I could hear the roaring of
the crowd.

"Stop running through the
house with your cleats on!"

I jogged out to the fifty-yard line. My cleats were squelching into the turf. Scott swung his bike around the side of the house. He was in his full uniform, too. Who could beat us?

Chapter 2
The Warm-up

I picked up the football and we jogged off. We ran twice around the lemon tree and once around the chicken coop.

A beautiful pass hit Scott in the chest. He looked surprised.

"Great catch," I yelled.

Scott punted the ball.

It sailed through the air and landed in the lemon tree.

"You'll have to climb up and get it!" I said.

"No way. It's your football, you get it," Scott yelled.

"No. You kicked it. You get it!" I snapped.

"I'm not playing on your team anymore," he shouted.

"That's fine," I said. "I didn't want you to play for the Topdogs anyway."

"I'm going to play for the Underdogs," he shouted. "They're the better team!"

So, the teams were set for the game. The real question was, what were we going to do for a ball?

Chapter 3
The Toss

Toocool to the rescue.

I grabbed a rake and asked Dad to knock the ball out of the tree. Then I split a rotten lemon for the toss. Scott got to call it because he was the visiting team.

"Flat side you win, round side I win," I said.

The lemon splattered as it accidentally hit Scott's head.

"I win," I said quickly. "Your team's going for the goal line at the chicken coop. My team will go for the garage."

We got into our positions.
The crowd was silent. We
eyeballed each other for the
kickoff. The ball was in play.
So were we.

I kicked the ball past Scott.
I leaped over him to catch my
own kick. I threw the
ball in for a perfect
touchdown pass.

"Six to nothing" I yelled.

"No way—it was incomplete!" Scott said. I knew I was right.

I got ready to kick in the extra point I had coming to me. I felt a thud on the back of my head. Scott had thrown a lemon at me!

"Penalty! That was an illegal procedure," I said.

"Who made you the referee?" Scott yelled.

15

Now Scott's team had the
ball. Scott was so mad he tried
to kick a field goal. Instead of
going over the chicken coop,
the ball went straight through
the coop's door.

Bert the Rooster bolted
out. Now the game was
getting good.

The Topdogs needed another touchdown to be safe. Scott and I faced off again. I pretended to throw a pass. Then I tucked the ball under my arm and ran hard. Scott was about to tackle me. Could I make it? I reached the goal as he grabbed me.

As I fell, the ball flew through the open door of the garage. Six cans of paint crashed to the ground. Oops.

Chapter 4
The Fight

Scott was playing well. He had played himself into field goal position and was ready to score.

"End of quarter," I said quickly.

"No way!" Scott yelled. "We just got started."

"Hey, the quarter's over. The clock doesn't lie."

The team benches emptied
onto the field. Six chickens
and Dog tried to line up. Bert
the Rooster stayed back in
the stands.

The second quarter began. Scott was determined to run in for a touchdown. I charged him, and tackled hard. Down he went. I tried to intercept the ball, but Scott tackled me.

"Five-yard penalty!" he said.

"For what?" I asked.

"Holding. You grabbed me while the ball was in play."

"No, I didn't."

"Yes, you did."

Scott pushed me. I pushed him back. It was the first fight of the game.

We rolled in the mud. I had a mouthful of grass and dirt.

Suddenly, the rest of our teams got involved. Dog jumped on top of us. He grabbed Scott's shoelace and pulled.

Everyone was yelling.

"Boys! Stop fighting and come in here for lunch," Mom shouted.

This time Scott admitted it was halftime. We ate a whole plate of sandwiches before the second half. I thought about my game.

It was time to get serious. The Topdogs needed me. I just hoped that those sandwiches wouldn't slow me down.

Chapter 5
Interception!

Third quarter. Scott had the ball. He was running when he slipped in the mud. The ball flew into the air, and I grabbed it. I raced for the end zone.

Scott made his second great
tackle of the day. As he threw
me down, I fumbled the ball.
Scott tried to grab it but he
was too late.

Dog grabbed the ball and
ran. Interception! Dog headed
for the garage. I ran to the left
and Scott ran to the right. We
dived at Dog. Dog ducked.
Splat! Scott and I crashed.

We sat looking at each other. Scott was rubbing his head. My nose started to bleed. Bert the Rooster crowed. Scott and I agreed that this meant it was the fourth quarter. We staggered to our huddles.

Chapter 6
The Clock Runs Out

The crowd roared. It was the final quarter. Scott grabbed the ball. I tackled him. When the ball bounced away, I snatched it up. I ran it in for a touchdown.

Another six points! The crowd exploded with noise. Toocool had come to life!

I immediately completed a perfect kick and scored the extra point. Scott didn't know what had hit him. He couldn't even remember if he was playing offense or defense. Soon, I had scored another four touchdowns. The clock ticked down, and the game was over. The crowd went crazy.

I ran around the field, waving my lucky jersey over my head.

The brutal football season was over. Toocool, most valuable player of the game, had just won another Super Bowl!

What would be next? Toocool, champion cyclist, races to a new world record?

The End!

Toocool's
Football Glossary

Field goal—Kicking the ball across the goal line and between the goalposts at the end of the field. Scores three points.

Huddle—When the players crowd together to plan what they're going to do, it's called a huddle.

Interception—When a player from the defensive team gets the ball away from the team that is trying to score.

Touchdown—Running the ball across the goal line, or catching a ball that has been thrown over the goal line. Scores six points.

Toocool's Backyard
Champion Stadium

Kitchen

Toocool's
Locker
Room

Living
Room

31

Toocool's Quick Summary
Football

Football is one of the most popular sports played in the United States. People started playing football in the mid-1800s, and today, millions of people watch their favorite teams play every autumn.

Football teams can have many players, but only eleven players from each team can play at a time.

The offense is the team that has the ball and is trying to score.

The defense is the team that is trying to keep the other team from scoring. The offense can score by running or passing the ball down the field and across the other team's goal line.

If they get the ball across the goal line, they score a touchdown, which is six points. If they kick the ball through the goalpost at the goal line, they score a field goal, which is three points.

If a team scores, the ball goes to the other team. Each football player has a special skill. Some are fast. Some can throw the ball really well. Others are strong at blocking runners and tackling.

Because football can be a rough sport, the players have to look out for each other besides doing their own job on the field. All of these players have to work together to win games.

The **Stadium**

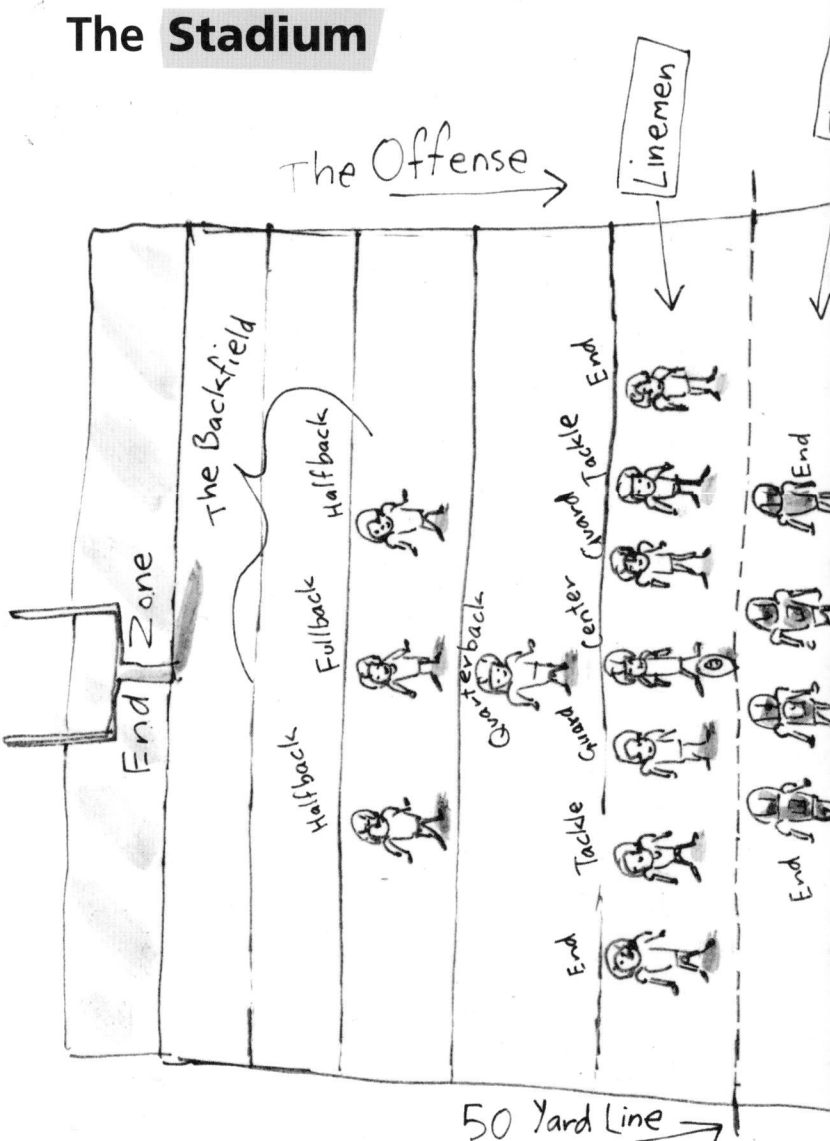

The Offense →

Linemen

The Backfield

End Zone

Halfback

Fullback

Halfback

Quarterback

Center

Guard

Tackle

End

Guard

Tackle

End

End

End

50 Yard Line →

34

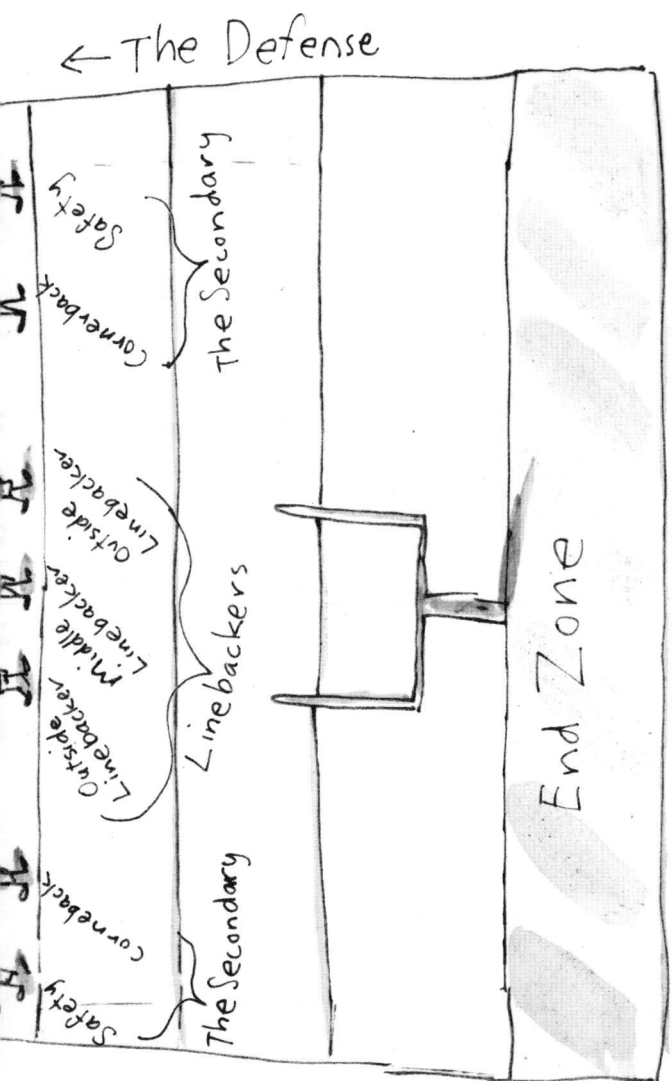

← The Defense

The Secondary

Safety

Cornerback

Linebackers

Outside Linebacker

Middle Linebacker

Outside Linebacker

The Secondary

Cornerback

Safety

End Zone

35

Q & A with Toocool
He Answers His Own Questions

Do the best players get to wear a number 1 on their jersey, or do they get to wear any number they like?

Football players can only choose from numbers that no other player is using. Sometimes, if a player is really great, his number will be retired. This means that no one on the team can ever use his number again. I have a feeling that when I stop playing football, my number will be retired, not just by my team, but by the whole league.

What should football players do before a game?

Get dressed. Football players owe it to their fans to make sure they show up on the field looking tough and ready. Strap on your helmet. Put on the pads, because this is a game that will crunch your bones. It's also a good idea to double knot the laces on your cleats, because you don't want to run out of your shoes during a big game.

What should football players do after a game?

When you're a great player like I am, all of the reporters always want to talk to you after a game. If I haven't thought up something really smart to say, I tell knock knock jokes. I also make sure my hair looks really good for the photos.

What makes you such a football legend?

Well, most players are known for playing only one position. I truly am a great quarterback, because I can plan just what my team needs to do to win. I'm very fast. I also throw the ball farther and better than anyone. Still, what makes me really great is that I can also catch the ball, intercept the ball, and tackle the other team. Very few players are tough and smart enough to do all these things.

What do you do after you win a game?

I like to shake the hands of every player on the other team. Oh, and then I have to ride around on the shoulders of my teammates.

What do you do after you lose a game?

I don't know. I've never lost a game before.

Football Quiz
How Much Do You Know about Football?

Q1 If your team scores 4 touchdowns, 3 conversions, and a field goal, how many points would they have scored?
A. 22. **B.** 30. **C.** 23.

Q2 What is the kickoff?
A. When you push your bike off the curb. **B.** When you kick the ball out of the field. **C.** When you kick the ball at the start of the game.

40

Q3 What is a conversion?

A. Three points, that are scored after a tackle. **B.** One point, that is scored after a touchdown. **C.** Six points, that are scored after an interception.

Q4 How many players from a team can be on the field at a time?

A. 9. **B.** 11. **C.** 16.

Q5 If a referee throws a yellow flag during a play, what has happened?

A. He has lost his hankie.

B. Someone has scored an extra point. **C.** Someone has done something wrong and earned a penalty.

Q6 What happens to a team that has done something wrong?
A. They have to move back on the field. **B.** They lose points.
C. They have to go home.

Q7 "Holding" means:
A. Grabbing onto a player from the other team. **B.** Comforting a team member. **C.** Gripping the ball tightly.

Q8 Who is the best football player in the world?
A. Dog. **B.** Bert. **C.** Toocool.

Q9 What is the draft?
A. The time when football teams get to pick new players. **B.** A cold blast of air. **C.** A large horse.

Q10 Why do football players wear black grease under their eyes? *A.* To look mean and scary. *B.* To annoy their moms. *C.* To help them see in the bright light.

ANSWERS

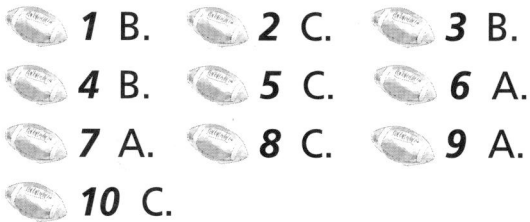

1 B.   *2* C.   *3* B.

4 B.   *5* C.   *6* A.

7 A.   *8* C.   *9* A.

10 C.

If you got ten questions right, you can join Toocool in the Topdogs. If you got more than five right, you can get a spot in the Underdogs with Scott. If you got fewer than five right, maybe you should play marbles.

Too Cool

Sonic Mountain Bike

It's a race against time.
Luckily, **Toocool** is a
speed machine. Nothing
will stop him from
breaking the paper-route
record. Or will it?

Titles in the Toocool series